Disciples Redeemed

A Dramatic Commemoration
Of The Last Supper

Raymond I. Keffer

CSS Publishing Company, Inc.
Lima, Ohio

DISCIPLES REDEEMED

Copyright © 1995 by
CSS Publishing Company, Inc.
Lima, Ohio

You may copy the material in this publication if you are the original purchaser, for use as it was intended (worship material for worship use; educational material for classroom use; dramatic material for staging and production). No additional permission is required from the publisher for such copying by the original purchaser only. Inquiries should be addressed to: CSS Publishing Company, Inc., 517 South Main Street, P.O. Box 4503, Lima, Ohio 45802-4503.

ISBN 0-7880-0373-9   PRINTED IN U.S.A

*To my wife Gail Keffer
　　son Rhett Keffer, Sr., and his wife Dana
　　grandsons Rhett, Jr., and Ross*

Table Of Contents

Preface	7
Saul Of Tarsus	9
James, The Younger	10
Simon Peter	11
Jude Thaddeus	13
Thomas	14
Andrew	15
James, The Elder	16
Philip	17
Nathaniel	18
Matthew	19
Simon, The Zealot	20
John	22
Judas (*Optional*)	23
Paul	24
Staging	26
Acknowledgements	28

Preface

This is a series of monologues about the lives of the Disciples of Christ following His death, resurrection, and ascension into Heaven. There is no time period for this series; it's just a collection of the events in their lives until all but one had met a tragic death. The disciples are brought together in the setting of the Last Supper so each can relate his own story to us. Saul, later known as Paul, is used to tie together the stories of these men who risked everything to spread the Good News of Jesus, and who, all but Judas, were redeemed by Jesus.

Jesus spoke to them, saying, "I am the light of the world; he who follows me will not walk in darkness, but will have the light of life."

— John 8:12 (RSV)

Saul Of Tarsus

"I am Saul of Tarsus. Like my fellow Jews, I am a true believer in the God of Abraham, Isaac, and Jacob. I have a commission from the leaders of the one true church to eliminate a troublesome group known as Christians, the followers of Jesus of Nazareth; the same Jesus who was crucified for His false teachings. I intend to give these Christians the same punishment for blasphemy Stephen got: death by stoning. This threat to the one true religion and to the one true God, Jehovah, cannot be ignored any longer. I'm on my way to Damascus to begin this work to cleanse the world of this foul group known as Christians."

(*EXIT — Bright lights*) "Saul, why are you persecuting me?"

James, The Younger

"I am James, son of Alphaeus, brother of Matthew. Following the resurrection and ascension of Jesus, I gathered with my fellow disciples in this room for we were all unsure as to what our future was to be since Christ was no longer here to lead us. I was elected spokesman for the group. We knew being followers of Jesus that our lives were in danger as people like Saul of Tarsus were lurking about to have us put to death.

"We heard of the conversion of Saul on the road to Damascus, and of his new zeal to preach the Gospel of Christ using the new name of Paul. When Paul appeared before us in Jerusalem, I was moved by the Holy Spirit to welcome him as a fellow Christian. I pleaded his case before the disciples that we should commission Paul to carry the good news of Jesus into the Gentile world.

"While the other disciples were called to preach the Gospel in other parts of the world, I stayed in Jerusalem, to become, as Paul said, a pillar of the new church of Jesus Christ. I faced death daily by witnessing for my Lord. One day while preaching in the temple in Jerusalem, I was attacked by a mob. I was taken to a pinnacle of the temple and thrown onto the rocks below, where washers of clothes bashed in my skull, tore at my body, and broke my bones. I willingly died for Jesus who has died so that we all might live."

Simon Peter

"I am Peter, a simple fisherman until Jesus made me a fisher of men. I did not fully understand what a 'fisher of men' was until Jesus had risen from the dead and had ascended into Heaven. For after these events, the Holy Spirit breathed on me that Pentecost Sunday morning and filled me and others with His inner presence. Then I began to speak out boldly for Jesus and His kingdom in a voice that every person could understand in his native tongue. Pentecost was a miracle.

"With the zeal of the Holy Spirit, I traveled the known world with longer stays in Greece. It was in Greece that I learned, that as a Christian, I must put aside my strict Jewish upbringing. This upbringing caused me to abandon my Greek Christian friends when Greek Jews came to dinner. Much to my embarrassment and shame I learned that we are all one in Christ, Jew and Gentile alike.

"After Greece, I continued my preaching and teaching until I arrived in Rome, the very heart of the Empire. I was able to win many souls for Christ in Rome before being arrested. I was charged with treason and placed in a darkened jail cell. I was not to see the light of day for nine months. I was never alone in that darkness. The Holy Spirit ministered unto me as I ministered to those jailed with me. After nine months, I was taken from my cell to be crucified. I asked to be crucified upside down as I was not worthy to die in the same manner as my Master had died.

"I was sustained on the cross by the words of Jesus who said: 'I will give you the keys of the Kingdom.' He did."

Jude Thaddeus

"I am Jude Thaddeus. I am often referred to as both Jude and Thaddeus. I was the first missionary. My travels took me to Syria, Persia, and Russia. My commission to spread the gospel came from the Garden of Gethsemane.

"All of us were in that Garden when I asked Jesus why He had revealed Himself to us only and not to the whole world. Jesus answered, 'If a man loves me and keeps my word, my Father and I will love him and We will come to him and abide in him.' I didn't understand the full meaning of these words until Pentecost. I knew then I had to carry His gospel to the world so that our triune God, Father, Son, and Holy Spirit, could abide in others as they abided in me. My preaching burst forth with the good news like a pot of hot water boiling over a hot fire.

"I lived among the non-Christians of the world and won many souls for Christ until my martyred death in Syria. A mob led by idol-worshiping priests attacked me while I was preaching the good news. I was tied to a cross to die a slow, painful death. As I hung on that cross, the indwelling God did not forsake me. I was comforted by Him on my journey into His kingdom."

Thomas

"I am Thomas, a pessimist, doubter, and unhappy person until Jesus changed my life. Following the death of Jesus, I was frightened and grieved for Jesus. We all did. When the news came of His rising from the dead, I refused to believe this news until I saw Him in the flesh with my own eyes. I was criticized for my doubting.

"While in this room, Jesus suddenly appeared to us, and I fell on my knees and cried out, 'My Lord and my God.' Understanding my doubts Jesus placed my hand into His side. He placed my fingers into His nail holes so that I and other doubters would believe. I no longer doubted.

"Filled with the Holy Spirit, I became a fearless carrier of the good news of Jesus. I traveled from Babylon to India. In India, I labored long as a builder of Christ's church. Jews and Gentiles alike accepted Jesus as their Savior. One day while building a new church, we were attacked by non-believers and a lance pierced my body. I did not die alone as Jesus was with me as I walked through the valley of the shadow of death. Glory be to God for the life He gave me free of doubt."

Andrew

"I am Andrew, brother of Peter, a 'fisher of men.' I first was a follower of John the Baptist, until Christ called me to put down my fishing nets and to follow Him. It was after the ascension of Jesus that I began my labor for Him. I picked up my cross to follow in His path.

"All my Christian brothers here fled Jerusalem to avoid persecution and death, that is all of us but James. He stayed. Had we not fled from here, the world would not have known of the sacrifices Christ made for us and for them, the unsaved. After Pentecost, I preached and taught in the nations of Macedonia and Greece. The Lord blessed my work. Everywhere I preached, converts were made. I was stoned and driven from some towns by my fellow Jews and idol worshipers. I praised God for allowing me to suffer on His behalf, for He promised that if we suffered for Him, we would share a room in His mansion in Heaven with Him forever.

"I tried to live my life as a testimony to Jesus. Although my death was one of agony, my testimony for Jesus continued until I had taken my last breath. I was crucified on an X-shaped cross, not the traditional cross like Jesus. I was tied to this cross for two days before I died.

"Praise God for His blessings and for His amazing grace that saved a wretched sinner like me."

James, The Elder

"I am James, son of Zebedee. I was one of the three disciples, along with Peter and John, who were the closest to Jesus. We were with Him when he raised Jairus' daughter from the dead, when the transfiguration took place, and the night of his betrayal in the Garden. I was there to share both His glory and His sorrow. When He died on that cross for me, He conquered death for me by rising from the dead. How better to serve Him than by telling others in the world of His sacrifice and redemption?

"I knew that winning others to Christ would not be easy, but Jesus had said, 'Lo I am with you always, even until the end of the world.' Armed with His promise and the power of the Holy Spirit, I set out to speak boldly for Jesus. I preached to Jews that Jesus was the fulfillment of the Scriptures. To the Gentiles I preached that the good news of salvation through Jesus was open to all who would confess Him as their Lord and Savior.

"I traveled all around the Mediterranean Sea even to Sardinia and Spain. God gave me successes wherever I preached.

"I became the first of the disciples to die. My preaching became a threat to a local pagan ruler. I was arrested and taken to the executioner where I was beheaded. With one swing of the sword, my earthly life came to an end. But Jesus was the keeper of my soul. I am with Him and my friends."

Philip

"I am Philip. Unlike the others here, I am a Jew of Greek background. Jesus cried out to me one day, 'Follow Me.' I did and brought Nathaniel with me. I introduced Greeks to Jesus; many became His devoted followers. I was there when He fed the 5000 from a small boy's fishes and loaves of bread. I hid at the time of Calvary, but after Jesus rose from the dead, I was willing to take any risk to win others for Christ. Death had lost its sting with the victory of Jesus on the cross.

"Being of Greek background, I preached and worked among the Greeks for 20 fruitful years. One day while walking, I came upon a serpent idol worship service. In the name of the cross, I commanded the worship to stop. The dying serpent gave off a gas so powerful that it killed many worshipers, including the king's son. In the name of Jesus, I prayed over the dead son and life was restored to him. The king became a convert, but other followers of the serpent attacked me. I was tied to a cross and stoned to death. While on the cross, I praised God and prayed for my murderers to see the light. Some of the murderers were won over for Christ as a result. With my last breath, I commended my spirit into God's hands as my Master did before He died."

Nathaniel

"I am Nathaniel. I was with Philip when he was attacked and crucified, but I managed to escape. I did not know why I was spared while Philip died. I agonized over the death of my friend, Philip, but I knew I must continue our mission to spread the saving grace that God provided man through Jesus.

"My missionary work took me to many lands including Russia, Persia, and India. I carried copies of the Gospel of Matthew with me. In India copies were left with Jews so that they could learn of Jesus through the written word. Like the others here, I too was hounded in every town by fellow Jews and idol worshipers.

"Despite all, my ministry took hold. I could witness to people about Jesus because I knew Him both as a personal friend and as my personal Savior. My death came about one day while I was healing the daughter of a king. In the name of Jesus, I healed the daughter of her lunacy which resulted in the king and others there coming to accept Christ. But the king's idol-worshiping brother had me arrested.

"I was given a trial, mocked, and placed on a cross where I was clubbed to death. Dying, I prayed to God to forgive them as Jesus forgave his murderers."

Matthew

"I am Matthew, son of Alphaeus, brother of James. I was blessed as only one other disciple was blessed. I was given the honor of writing a Gospel which told of the life of our Lord Jesus. I wrote of how He fulfilled the scriptures of old, and how God has offered salvation through His Son, Jesus. What more honor would one want in a lifetime than to write such a book?

"I was further blessed by being able to witness to my fellow men in many nations of the world. Worldly riches were nothing. I knew firsthand that riches stored up in Heaven were greater than any riches stored up on Earth. For until Jesus changed my life, I was a tax collector. Riches were everything.

"My death came by an act of a jealous king. He was jealous of my security in Christ. He wanted my security, but he wouldn't surrender himself to Jesus. This king tied me up, placed me on sticks of wood, and covered my body with oil-soaked papyrus. Worse than that, he insulted God by surrounding me with 12 false gods. When he lit my funeral fire, I commanded the fire to consume the 12 false gods, which it did. As I prayed for the souls of my oppressors, the king asked for forgiveness and was saved through Christ. By now my torment was such that I asked the Lord to take my soul and free me from this suffering. He did. I now share eternity with Jesus."

Simon, The Zealot

"I am Simon the Zealot, a zealot who wanted the world to be good and perfect, but who did not know how to make it so. I became a follower of Jesus at an age much older than these men. I did not know peace and love until I had surrendered all to Jesus. I, like the others, was unsure what plans God had for me following the ascension of Jesus. I became fully aware of these plans after Pentecost. The Holy Spirit filled me with the desire to tell others of the love of Jesus and the gift of life He offered them. Jesus taught us that He was the Way, the Truth, and the Life, and that no one reached the Father except through Him.

"I had to share this message among the lost souls of the world. My witnessing took me throughout the known world including the British Isles. My labor of love among the lost souls was not easy; however, God blessed my work everywhere I went. The truth of the Gospel was able to penetrate even the most tough-minded societies. The Roman Empire had provided me the means by which I could travel throughout the many conquered lands.

"All of us here joyously harkened to the command of Jesus to spread His gospel unto the edges of the Earth.

"My exposure to the Romans eventually led to my death at their hands. I was arrested for treason and crucified on a cross. I deemed it an honor to die as my Master had died; the Romans could not understand my peace. I died before them not begging for mercy, but praying for their souls. Jesus' love had conquered me so that I could now pray for the once-hated Romans."

John

"I am John, the last of the disciples to die. From the cross, Jesus commanded me to take care of His mother, Mary, which I did. He had other tasks for me to carry out for Him as well. I, like Matthew, was blessed to write one of the Gospels.

"I did not know until after Pentecost why Jesus had named me and my brother, Sons of Thunder. But after Pentecost, we were armed with the power of the Holy Spirit, and we thundered the good news to both Jew and Gentile alike. I preached that God so loved the world that He gave His only begotten Son so that the world might not perish, but have everlasting life through His son, Jesus.

"I ministered throughout Greece, but I spent a lot of time in Ephesus. I wrote letters to other churches, preached the Gospel and taught others to be ministers for Jesus. My working for Jesus got me exiled by a jealous Greek ruler to an island off Greece. I was to perform hard labor there, but God had other plans for me.

"I received many revelations from God which I put into a book for mankind to read and to study. When the jealous ruler died, I returned to Ephesus where I lived a long life and died a natural death. My life was blessed like no other disciple's life, which is why I am referred to as John the Beloved."

Judas
(Optional)

"I am Judas. I was once one of them, but I refused to listen to what Jesus was teaching us. I betrayed Jesus because I did not listen. I was selfish, greedy, and spiteful. I wanted a kingdom on this earth — a kingdom now, on my terms, with me in a powerful position. I wanted people to look up to me and to hold me in awe. How wrong I was.

"I realized too late what I had done by betraying Jesus. I gave back the 30 pieces of silver. I tried to call the whole deal off, but the priests would have none of it. I betrayed the one who loved me with a kiss. I caused Him to die on the cross.

"The agony of these selfish acts drove me to take my own life with this rope. I am among the lost which Satan now claims as his own. If only I had listened to Jesus. If only I had died to self as He asked me to do. Since I did not listen to Jesus, I now must spend eternity in despair and lament. Woe unto me, a sinner who has received his just reward."

Paul

(Last to speak after John, [or Judas, if used])
"I am Paul. When I appeared before these disciples to attest to my conversion to Christianity, James, son of Alphaeus, the spokesman for the disciples, welcomed me. He tried to remove doubts that these disciples still had about me by telling of my adherence to Mosaic Laws in all my preaching and works. The others were moved by the Holy Spirit and accepted me. I was commissioned by them to work with the Gentiles following the commands of Jesus to minister in His name throughout the world.

"I visited the nations around the Mediterranean Sea. For Jesus I won many souls, planted many seeds, established churches, wrote letters, and sent emissaries to make sure that the seeds and churches took root and grew.

"However, all was not easy. I was beaten, jailed, stoned and shipwrecked in my efforts to spread the Gospel. I was even threatened with death, but being a Roman citizen, only a trial in Rome itself could bring a sentence of death. Once in Rome, death did not come before I preached and won souls for Christ there.

"Finally, by order of the emperor, I was beheaded. Death was quick and painless as compared to what these men endured. I was prepared for death. I knew that I had run the good race; I had fought the good fight; I had kept the faith. Gladly I had suffered the hurts, imprisonments, despair, and loneliness for Jesus, as my suffering was nothing compared to His suffering. As we were all persecuted for Jesus and our faith, we shall all spend eternity with Him. Jesus kept His promise. *We are redeemed.*"

Staging

The staging of the *Disciples Redeemed* can be done on a stage with a table set up like the last supper table with the disciples, except for Judas, seated around the table. The story begins with Saul giving his monologue at floor level with the audience. The disciples sit with their eyes cast downward until Saul has exited and has been faced with the light, stage left. (This young Saul wears a wig and is not bearded.)

James, son of Alphaeus, begins. If you are using Judas, then each disciple exits after his speech and a white stole is placed around his neck. Judas appears at audience level with a rope around his neck and speaks with the stage empty. After Judas exits, Paul appears on stage to be greeted first by James, son of Alphaeus, then the others prior to retaking their seats. An older Paul then moves to stage right, in front of the table, to deliver his speech. (Paul also is wearing a white stole like the disciples, is bearded, and bald, if possible.) Everyone is dressed in clothing of the Biblical time period. Judas does not appear with the others at this time.

It is suggested that you use the hymn, "My Tribute" by Andrae Crouch in the devotional prior to the presentation. "My Tribute" sets the mood nicely for *Disciples Redeemed*. The refrain is then used effectively after Paul says, "We are redeemed!" as Paul raises his arms in praise to God while the refrain is being sung from backstage. Paul then takes a seat at the table with the disciples.

Should you choose not to use Judas, have the disciples wear their white stoles and remain on stage the entire time. After John, then have James, son of Alphaeus, rise to greet Paul as he enters. Paul then moves to stage front right to give his speech.

The scripture recommended as part of the devotional with "My Tribute," is Matthew 28:16-20.

The order of the disciple's testimony follows the order they are presented in the script. Saul begins, and Paul ends the testimony.

If desired, a communion service may be held after the presentation with those elders who are participating serving the elements.

An option for use of these monologues is to present one monologue at each of the mid-week and Sunday services during Lent beginning with Ash Wednesday and concluding with the Maundy Thursday service.

Acknowledgements

The *Disciples Redeemed* is dedicated to The Rev. Dr. Velis Vais, pastor of the Clen Moore Presbyterian Church whose sermon on the deaths of the disciples stirred me to write their stories in monologue form, to the McGill P.C.C. Board, to the Tri-M Bible School Class, to my wife Gail, and to the men who put their lives at risk so that we all might better know the good news of Jesus.